World's Cutest PUPPIES

in 3-D

by Katie McConnaughey

SCHOLASTIC

New York · Toronto · London · Auckland
Sydney · Mexico City · New Delhi · Hong Kong

World's Cutest Puppies in 3-D produced by becker&mayer!
11120 NE 33rd Place, Suite 101
Bellevue, WA 98004
www.beckermayer.com

ISBN 978-0-545-27423-4

10 9 8 7 6 5 4 3 2 1   10 11 12 13 14

Printed in Dongguan, China
First printing, September 2010

10758

Written by Katie McConnaughey
Edited by Betsy Henry Pringle
Designed by Rosanna Brockley
3-D anaglyph effects by Matthew Fisher
Photo research by Zena Chew
Production management by Larry Weiner

Photo credits: Front cover: Yorkshire terrier puppy © Eric Isselée/Shutterstock; English bulldog puppy © jhorrocks/iStockphoto; Golden retriever puppy © Pieter/Shutterstock. Title page: Golden retriever puppies © vgm/Shutterstock. Page 3: Fluffy puppy © Aneta Blaszczyk/stock.xchng. Page 4: Kadi © 2009 Back in the Pack Dog Portraits. Page 5: Chaz and toy © Joe Elliott; Rhodesian ridgebacks © Clarissa Leahy/Photographer's Choice/Getty Images. Page 6: Beagle puppy © Waldemar Dabrowski/Shutterstock. Page 7: Whiskey © Jennifer Singerman; Maltese puppy © Jello5700/iStockphoto. Page 8: Hungarian vizsla © Ákos Váradi. Page 9: Havanese puppies © PJ Taylor/Flickr/Getty Images; Magyar Agar © Picani Picani/Photolibrary. Page 10: Tucker © 2009 BITP. Page 11: Labrador and boots © LynetteJ/iStockphoto; Puppy and horse © Somogyvari/iStockphoto. Page 12: Golden retriever puppies © Juniors Bildarchiv/Photolibrary. Page 13: Beagle puppies © Juniors Bildarchiv/Photolibrary; Tommy © BITP. Page 14: French bulldog puppy © Kalvis Kalsers/Dreamstime. Page 15: Chihuahua puppies © Juniors Bildarchiv/Photolibrary; Chaz on the stairs © Joe Elliott. Page 16: Sleepy terrier © Lisa Turay/iStockphoto. Page 17: Golden retriever puppy © Mike Thorn/stock.xchng; Two sleeping puppies © by_nicholas/iStockphoto. Page 18: Dachshund puppies © Datacraft/Getty Images. Page 19: Boxer puppies © cynoclub/Shutterstock; Irish setter puppies © Pixbilder/Dreamstime. Page 20: Oslo © Christiano Montiani. Page 21: Cosmo © 2009 BITP; Japanese chin puppy in garden © jhorrocks/iStockphoto. Page 22: Milly © Tony Harrison; Jake © 2009 BITP. Page 23: English springer spaniel puppy © appletat/iStockphoto; Pug puppy © joaniemary/Flickr/Getty Images. Page 24: German shepherd puppy © pailoolom/iStockphoto. Page 25: Yorkshire terrier puppy © scorpp/iStockphoto; Pug puppy eating © Juniors Bildarchiv/Photolibrary. Page 26: Delilah the blue Dane © David Boyd. Page 27: Newton © 2009 BITP; Chihuahua puppies © Anna Utekhina/Dreamstime. Page 28: Dylan © Scott Beckner. Page 29: Maltese puppies © Pixmann Limited/Photolibrary; Beagle puppy © Eric Isselée/Shutterstock. Page 30: Dachshund puppy © Sharon Montrose/Stone/Getty Images. Page 31: Olwen © Mike Bostock; French bulldog puppy © Denise Kappa/iStockphoto. Page 32: Weimaraner puppy © Kristina Jackson/Flickr/Getty Images. Page 33: Bluetick coonhound puppy © burbee/iStockphoto; St. Bernard puppy © ghprincess/stock.xchng. Page 34: Dachshund © Duccio/Dreamstime. Page 35: Puppy in action © Rashard I. Kelly; Rhodesian ridgeback puppy © Nancy Dressel/Dreamstime. Page 36: Romeo © Sarah Mitchell. Page 37: Terrier puppy © Pavel Sazonov/Dreamstime; Beagle puppy © Lars Sundström/stock.xhng. Page 38: Yorkshire terrier puppy © Cheryl E. Davis/iStockphoto. Page 39: Chihuahua puppy © Kelly Richardson/iStockphoto; Chihuahua puppy © Altrendo Images/Getty Images. Page 40: Pepper © Evan Agee. Page 41: Dogue de Bordeaux puppy © vitalytitov/iStockphoto; Bulldog puppy © Ben Conlan/iStockphoto. Page 42: Welsh corgi puppies © DAJ/Getty Images. Page 43: Cleo and Sophie © 2009 BITP; Shar-pei puppies © cooleer/iStockphoto. Page 44: Golden retrievers © GK Hart/Vikki Hart/Stone/Getty Images. Page 45: Boston terriers © BITP/Flickr/Getty Images; Pit bull terrier family © zamanyahre/iStockphoto. Page 46: Fury © Brandalynn Toews. Page 47: Luigi © BITP/Flickr/Getty Images; Ozzy © 2009 BITP. Page 48: Puppy smelling flower © Percent/Dreamstime. Back cover: Basset hound puppies © Eric Isselée/Shutterstock; Pug puppy © Utekhina Anna/Shutterstock; Labrador puppy © B. Scott Photography/iStockphoto; brown puppy © Fnsy/Shutterstock; Chihuahua puppy © Eric Isselée/Shutterstock.

The wonderful world of puppies

What is cuter than a puppy? Lots of puppies! Puppies come in all shapes and sizes, but they all like to play, chew, wrestle, and cuddle. This book takes you inside the world of puppies, and the 3-D glasses make it seem like the puppies are right there with you!

So punch out and assemble your 3-D glasses, turn the page, and jump into the wonderful world of puppies!

Oh, hello! Will you be my friend?

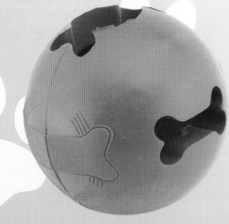

Puppies at Play

This chew toy makes a great headrest!

Toys! Toys! Toys!

Puppies are playful, and they're thrilled with any kind of toy you give them. A ball, a flying disc, or even a rope can keep a puppy busy for hours!

Just like Mom?

Puppies love playing with stuffed toys. Sometimes a puppy will shake or tear apart a stuffed animal. A puppy might also carry around a favorite stuffed animal in its mouth, the same way a mother dog carries her pup.

Do you want to play with my rabbit?

My brother and I love to wrestle!

Now THIS is fun!

It's always fun to play with a friend! When puppies wrestle or pounce on each other, they are usually playing, even though it may look like fighting. Puppies love to chase each other—it's like playing tag! Puppies like human playmates, too.

A Day at the Beach

Let's check out the beach!

Fun in the sun!

Going to the beach is a treat for a puppy. The warm sun on its fur, the sand beneath its paws, strange new smells, and the promise of a cool swim are all exciting. What a perfect day!

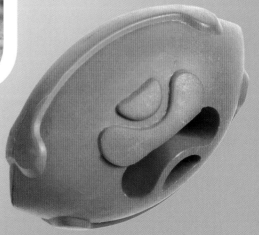

Taking in some rays

Before you head to the beach, check to see if your little friend is allowed to go with you. When you're packing the blanket and beach toys, don't forget to bring some fresh water and a water bowl—all that playing in the sun makes a puppy thirsty!

You don't mind that I took your blanket, do you?

Ready to play!

Special dog beaches allow dogs and puppies to roam freely on the sand and in the surf—as long as they obey their owners. Some dog beaches host hundreds of dogs at a time!

What shall we do first? Swim? Dig? Eat?

Let's Go to the Park!

The great outdoors

Puppies are full of energy and they need to play, so parks are perfect playgrounds for puppies. Active puppies may enjoy organized dog sports. Some sports teach puppies how to jump over hurdles and run through obstacle courses.

So the game is to stand on three legs—I mean, one leg—as long as you can.

Play ball!

Some dog parks let dogs run and play off-leash. But be careful—an active off-leash dog park might be overwhelming for a tiny puppy.

You guys stay here. I'll go get the ball!

Follow me!

A puppy can have fun at the park without toys or games. Just running makes a puppy happy!

Ha-ha! Just try to catch me now!

Hard at Work

Don't worry. I'll keep an eye on those sheep!

Guarding the sheep

Some puppies have jobs when they grow up! "Working dogs" help out their human friends in different ways. Herding dogs or sheepdogs help out on a farm by keeping track of larger animals such as sheep and cows.

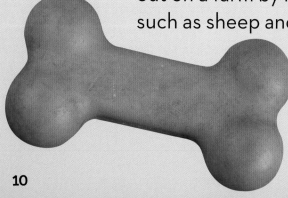

Watchdog

Some dogs are trained to make noise if the person or place they are guarding is threatened. Watchdogs bark, and guard dogs are trained to attack intruders. Instead of attacking, most young puppies will bark like watchdogs.

I'll bark nice and loud if anyone touches these boots!

At your service

Service puppies are trained to help people. Some grow up to be guide dogs for the blind. Therapy dogs become caring companions to people in hospitals and nursing homes. Therapy dogs are sometimes sent overseas to help soldiers feel a little closer to home.

Hi there. Can we be friends?

Let's Explore!

Follow me! The birds are right down here.

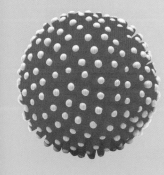

Come on!

Exploring is what puppies love best. If they get to chase birds and small animals, so much the better! Bird dogs are trained to hunt and catch birds. Retrievers like to bring you sticks, balls, or objects they have found.

Over, under, and through

Wriggling in and out of small places is fun for a puppy. Under the table, behind the sofa, through a drainage pipe—puppies never tire of exploring. And if a noisy vacuum cleaner or a thunderstorm scares a pup, these places are also good for hiding!

Where'd you get the leaf? I want a leaf . . .

Who's that?

When a puppy explores, it might catch its own reflection in a puddle, a mirror, or a window. Unlike you, the puppy doesn't realize that it is looking at itself in the surface, and it may start to bark—it thinks it sees another puppy!

See? I told you there was another puppy here!

Just Hanging Around the House

This is my favorite yoga position. Aren't I adorable?

Give it a rest!

Puppy owners can help their overactive puppies relax. Special yoga classes let owners and puppies pose and stretch together to become even better friends.

My new bed

A bed is a place where a puppy can nap and relax with a toy. A young puppy may miss the company of its mother, so sleeping in the bedroom with you can help your puppy feel safe.

Do you smell that? Is that pancakes?

Home alone

When puppies are left home alone, they can get into all sorts of trouble. Suddenly, what seemed like a sweet, harmless puppy is a naughty little disaster! A bored puppy might chew on shoes, unravel rolls of toilet paper, and tear up books.

Come on. Let me show you my toys.

Shhh . . . It's Nap Time!

Is it okay if I curl up and take a short nap?

Good night, sleep tight

Just like human babies, puppies need lots of sleep throughout the day. A healthy puppy may need fifteen or twenty hours of sleep every day! A puppy should go to bed early at night—like a baby—and wake up early.

A cuddly, sleepy friend

Puppies play hard while they are awake. And when they get sleepy, they nap hard, too. A puppy will curl up in its bed or on your lap and sleep, or it might just fall asleep on the floor!

The movie is good, but I can't quite . . . keep . . . my eyes . . . zzzzzzz.

All curled up

When given the chance, puppies will sleep curled up together to stay warm and feel safe. After all, they were used to being curled up with their mothers. Puppies can be taught to sleep by themselves, but most prefer the company of other animals.

Here. You be the pillow and I'll be the blanket!

Packs of Pups

We're ready for the movie now. Did you get the popcorn?

A group is better than one

A long time ago, before dogs began living and working with humans, they lived in packs. The pack is a social group, and, just like a family, pack members stick together and share everything.

Brothers and sisters

In a pack, both the mother and the father dog raise the puppies, all the dogs gather food, and they explore together. Nowadays, it's more common for only one or two dogs to live in any household.

Let's play king of the mountain!

Everyone say "Cheese!"

A litter of pups

A pack of puppies, or a litter, is a group of puppies that were born from the same mother at the same time. Having a group of brothers and sisters around gives a puppy 24-hour-a-day playmates!

Too Cool for School

This is my spot. You can't have it.

Mine!

All dogs, even puppies, are territorial. This means they protect their own space. Many puppies will claim the house and yard as their own. If a new person or another puppy enters that space, the puppy might get mad and bark like crazy or growl. Sometimes young puppies will protect a spot on the couch or their dinner bowl!

Little tough guy

Some small puppies tend to think they are bigger than they actually are. These puppies will act like big tough guard dogs or will try to carry items that are too heavy for them. Some try to bully much larger dogs.

You talking to me?

I'm in charge

In dog packs, one animal is the alpha—the leader of the group. A puppy will show it is the alpha when it doesn't obey or won't move out of the way. The message it is sending is "Even though I'm smaller than you, I'm still the one in charge!"

I'm serious. If you don't play with me, I can't let you through.

A Year of Pups

Sunny summer

I'm hot! Would you bring me some lemonade?

The days between July and early September are sometimes called the dog days of summer. Summer is a good time to get a puppy because school is out, so the puppy gets lots of attention.

Crisp autumn

Fall, or autumn, is marked by cooler weather and kids going back to school. It's a great time for a puppy to be outside. Many puppies love to play in the leaves or go for long walks. Some people dress up their puppies in Halloween costumes and take them out trick-or-treating!

Quick. Rake up the leaves again so I can jump in the pile!

Winter wonderland

Wintertime days are short and cold. Many animals hibernate for the winter, which means they sleep through most of the season. Dogs and puppies don't hibernate. In fact, many puppies love to play in the snow!

Let's build a snowdog!

Spring fever

After winter, spring is a welcome change for puppies. The days get longer, the air gets warmer, and there are lots of new smells to check out. Don't be surprised if a puppy starts sneezing after sniffing the fresh grass and spring buds!

Don't you just love spring? Everything is in bloom!

Chow Time!

This bone is bigger than I am!

Chewing all day long

Just like a baby, a puppy needs to chew on something while its larger adult teeth grow in. A sturdy bone is a great chew toy. Always make sure it is a bone made for a dog to chew. Some bones—like those from birds—can splinter and hurt a dog.

Chow down

A puppy starts to lose its puppy teeth when it is about four months old. Once adult teeth come in, the puppy will be able to chew almost anything. Dogs have strong teeth and jaws made for tearing meat. A large dog can bite about ten times harder than a human can!

Thanks! Dinner looks so good!

Oh, oops. Did you want some?

Good to the last drop!

Dogs can swallow much larger chunks of food than humans can, and puppies will sometimes "wolf down" their food, taking big gulps without even chewing. In addition to dog chow, puppies and dogs have been known to eat table scraps, pancakes, grass, and even dirt!

Look into My Eyes . . . ★ ★ ★

How could you ever say no to these eyes?

Sense of sight

Just like humans, puppies have five senses: sight, smell, taste, hearing, and touch. Because dogs are natural hunters, they can see well in dim light, while humans see better in bright light. Dogs are also good at detecting motion—a puppy can spot a tiny insect moving on the ground from far away.

Through a puppy's eyes

A puppy's eyes can come in many different colors, just like a human's: blue, green, black, and brown. But did you know that dogs have a third eyelid in the inner corner of each eye? This special eyelid blinks rapidly and helps keep the eye clean.

No . . . I swear I don't know where the cat is.

Seeing a different rainbow

Although you can see every color of the rainbow, dogs and puppies see fewer colors. Dogs' eyes see everything in shades of blue, yellow, and gray. To a dog, a red ball on green grass may look like a yellow ball on darker yellow grass.

You know that I love you, right?

Tongues and Tails

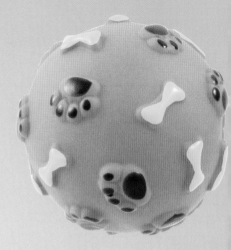

Mmm . . . that ice cream looks really good.

Slurp!

A puppy's tongue is one of the most important parts of its body. It's a powerful muscle that allows the puppy to lap water, lick food, and kiss playmates. Just like a human's tongue, a puppy's tongue is mostly used for tasting.

Pant, pant!

Dogs don't sweat when they get hot, nervous, or excited—they pant. When dogs pant, their tongues get bigger and often hang out of their mouths. Air moves across the tongue, cooling the whole body.

It's too hot to go for a run. Let's swim!

Wag that tail!

A puppy's tail lets humans know what the puppy is thinking or feeling. A wagging tail usually means "hello." A happy puppy's tail will be relaxed and in line with the ground—like the puppy in the photo. A scared puppy might start to shake, and its tail will be standing up or tucked between its hind legs.

See? I told you. It just kind of . . . moves . . . all on its own.

Ear! Ear!

Do you think I can fly with these things?

I'm all ears!

Newborn puppies can't hear. It takes about ten days for their ears to "open up." Once a puppy's ears are open, its hearing is better than a human's!

Did you call me?

Up and down

Puppy ears come in different sizes and shapes. Whether the ears are long and drooping, short and erect, or somewhere in between, they pick up sound vibrations that are traveling through the air and funnel them into the pup's eardrums.

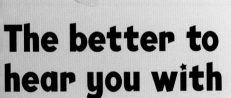

The better to hear you with

Dogs and puppies can hear sounds of a very high frequency. Humans can't hear sounds at this pitch. Sometimes puppies bark when humans hear or see nothing. This happens because the puppy hears something at a frequency beyond human range. The barking alerts humans to a possible threat.

You don't have to yell. I can hear you from here.

Those Feet!

High five!

These feet were made for walking

Unlike humans, who walk on the soles of their feet, puppies walk on their toes. The toes are padded to absorb the shock of the puppy's movement. A puppy's foot has four pads, each with its own claw, or toenail.

Quick! He went that way!

Running and jumping

Paws allow a puppy to explore the backyard, the park, the beach, and beyond! But puppy paws are for more than just walking. Puppy paws are for digging, running, jumping, and holding on to bones.

Paw prints

Some breeds of dogs have small, round feet. Other breeds have "hare feet," meaning that each foot has two long toes in the middle, like a rabbit's foot. Some dogs have webs between their toes—these make them good swimmers.

Ahh . . . let me just stretch out here.

The Nose Knows

Smell this one. Isn't it great?

Smells good!

Of its five senses, a puppy mostly uses its sense of smell. The part of the brain that deals with scent is almost 40 times bigger in a dog than it is in a human!

My nose knows the way. I'll take you there!

Cold and cute!

A puppy's nose is cold to the touch and slightly wet. A wet nose helps a puppy figure out what direction a smell comes from. If you have ever licked your finger to feel which way the wind is blowing, it's the same thing. The coldness helps cool the puppy down—just like panting does.

Sniff! Sniff!

A puppy's nose is extremely sensitive. Puppies can detect levels of scent almost 100 times lower than humans can. When a curious puppy explores, it may stop every few steps to sniff something you didn't even know had a smell!

You keep telling me to hurry up, but there are so many things to smell!

35

Rub My Belly

So if I roll over like this, then will you scratch my belly?

Belly up!

One of the most adorable things about a puppy is its squishy, soft belly. Most puppies love having their bellies rubbed simply because it feels good to them. When a puppy lets you rub its belly, it means that it trusts you.

I know you think I'm cute. Right? Don't you think I'm cute?

Cutie-pie

Not only are puppies cute, they are quick learners. If a human gives a puppy an order to sit and the puppy rolls over instead, it is because the puppy knows the human will rub its belly. Puppies know how to use their looks to get what they want!

Belly button

Puppies have belly buttons! When the puppy is a newborn, the belly button is visible. As the puppy gets older, the belly button shrinks to a tiny scar or a little fur-covered bump.

Ooh, I just love it when you rub my belly. Do it again.

So Tiny!

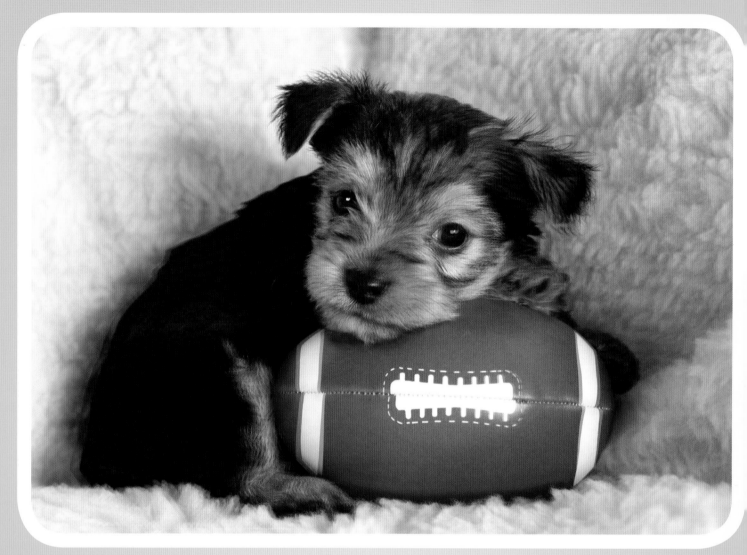

I would offer to go fetch this for you, but I don't think I can carry it.

Tiny friends

Very tiny breeds of dogs are called toy dogs. Dogs of this variety must weigh less than 22 pounds to be called toys. Some toy dogs weigh less than 8 pounds and stand less than 10 inches tall!

Small but mighty

Small dogs guard their turf just as fiercely as big dogs do. Many toy dogs are highly alert and hate having "their" property crossed by other dogs. Toy dogs will use their high, piercing barks to alert people to any threats. Some of the best watchdogs are dachshunds, Yorkshire terriers, poodles, and Boston terriers.

Yeah. I'm small. So what? I'm still tough.

Sweet, small, and smart

Many people choose small dogs if they have babies or young children at home. Puppies such as poodles, Shetland sheepdogs, Corgis, and Norwich terriers are quick learners and can be trained to respond well to small children or other pets.

I kept up my end of the deal. I got in the cup. Now I get a treat, right?

Funny Face

Yeah, I ate a fly. So what?

A face only a mother could love

People disagree about what puppies they find cute. Not everyone loves wrinkly little dogs like bulldogs or boxers. But these guys can be sweet, loyal friends for any family.

Wrinkles

While some people think wrinkly puppies aren't as cute as fluffy or furry puppies—others think wrinkly dogs are the best! Wrinkly-faced puppies sometimes need a bit of extra help cleaning their faces every day.

Are you laughing at my nose?

My mom says I'm beautiful. Do you think I am?

Bulldog buddies

Their wrinkly faces may make them look mean, but bulldogs are known to be good with babies and young children. Although they were originally meant for sporting, these dogs make great companions.

Friends Forever

This is Charlie. Can he stay for dinner?

Best buddies

Puppies are eager to make friends with people and other animals, but they like other puppies the best. When they see a potential puppy friend, puppies will wag their tails eagerly and bark in excitement.

Nope. I already told you. There's nothing in there.

Let me get that for you

Two or more puppies will groom, or clean, each other. This is called social grooming. Like cuddling, social grooming is a way of showing affection. If a puppy trusts its human friends, it might try to groom the humans, too!

Hey! You're almost as cute as I am!

Puppies love having another dog around the house. The other puppy will be a chum who is always around to play, wrestle, or cuddle with.

We do everything together.

My Family

Mommy and me

For the first few months of its life, a puppy learns a lot from its mother. The mother dog teaches her puppy how to eat, how to interact with other dogs, and even when it is okay to bark. If a puppy is taken from its mother too soon, it can't learn everything it needs to know to grow up to be the best dog it can be.

This is my mom.
Do you think she looks just like me?

He's my brother!

Even though puppies and dogs in a household might not be from the same parents, they live just like brothers or sisters. They might have different personalities, but they are usually the best of friends.

What do we do next, Spike? Eat?

Watch this!

Like human babies, puppies learn by watching the behavior of others in their families. Puppies can go to obedience school to learn to be good, but there are some things only a mother dog can teach her pup.

**So I look up and look cute . . .
just like this, right?**

Puppy Personalities

Let me explain it again. You throw this stick, and I'll go catch it.

Playful pooch

How do you know what kind of puppy is right for you? Do you like to run around and play a lot? If so, you might like a wild, energetic pup the best. These puppies will play all day, explore, and be part of any game you can imagine.

Supersweet

Instead of a playful puppy, you might prefer a less rambunctious pet. A lapdog will curl up with you when you read a book or watch TV. While still playful, less active puppies might suit you if you mostly want a friend that likes to cuddle.

I'll be here waiting for you!

You go ahead. I'm fine right here!

Lazy day

Some puppies are just plain lazy. They take lots of naps, play for only a short time, and are perfect little couch potatoes. They prefer to be alone, rather than in the company of others. A lazy, independent puppy could be the perfect pup for you if you have many friends and are often busy.

I love this flower. Can I pick it for you?

Ruff! Ruff! Bowwow!

Puppies may look and act differently, but some things about them are always true: They're fun, they need love and attention, and they'll be a friend for life.

With so many choices of furry friends—playful puppies, sleepy puppies, grumpy puppies, wrinkly puppies, big puppies, tiny puppies—which puppy would YOU choose to bring home?